D1627124

Nine

Fruits

of the

Spirit

A Bible Study on Developing Christian Character

Self-Control

Robert Strand

New Leaf Press
A Division of New Leaf Publishing Group

First printing: June 1999
Third printing: September 2009

ISBN-13: 978-0-89221-469-3
ISBN-10: 0-89221-469-4
Library of Congress Number: 99-64014

Cover by Janell Robertson

Printed in China

Please visit our website for other great titles:
www.newleafpress.net

For information regarding author interviews, please contact the publicity department at (870) 438-5288.

Contents

Introduction

There is an ancient story out of the Middle East which tells of three merchants crossing the desert. They were traveling at night in the darkness to avoid the heat of the day. As they were crossing over a dry creek bed, a loud attention-demanding voice out of the darkness commanded them to stop. They were then ordered to get down off their camels, stoop down and pick up pebbles from the creek bed, and put them into their pockets.

Immediately after doing as they had been commanded, they were then told to leave that place and continue until dawn before they stopped to set up camp. This mysterious voice told them that in the morning they would be both sad and happy. Understandably shaken, they obeyed the voice and traveled on through the rest of the night without stopping. When morning dawned, these three merchants anxiously looked into their pockets. Instead of finding the pebbles as expected, there were precious jewels! And, they were both happy and sad. Happy that they had picked up some of the pebbles, but sad because they hadn't gathered more when they had the opportunity.

This fable expresses how many of us feel about the treasures of God's Word. There is coming a day when we will be thrilled because we have absorbed as much as we have, but sad because we had not gleaned much more. Jewels are best shown off when held up to a bright light and slowly turned so that each polished facet can catch and reflect the light.

Each of these nine jewels of character will be examined in the light of God's Word and how best to allow them to be developed in the individual life. That is how I feel about the following three verses from Paul's writings which challenge us with what their Christian character or personality should look like. Jesus Christ has boiled down a Christian's responsibility to two succinct commands: Love the Lord your God with all your heart, mind, soul, and body, and love your neighbor like yourself. Likewise, Paul the apostle has captured for us the Christian personality in nine traits:

> But the fruit of the Spirit is love, joy, peace, patience, kindness, goodness, faithfulness, gentleness, and self-control. Against such things there is no law. Those who belong to Christ Jesus have crucified the sinful nature with its passions and desires. Since we live by the Spirit, let us keep in step with the Spirit (Gal. 5:22–25).

At the very beginning of this study, I must point out a subtle, yet obvious, distinction. The "fruit" of the Spirit is a composite description of what the Christian lifestyle and character traits are all about — an unbroken whole. We can't pick only the fruit we like.

Unlocked in these nine portraits are the riches of a Christ-centered personality. The thrill of the search is ahead of us!

Self-Control

ENKRATEIA, (Greek), meaning: *en*,
infused or within; *kratos*, vigor,
dominion, power, strength. Having a
great force within but under control.

*THE FRUIT OF THE
SPIRIT IS . . . SELF-CONTROL!*

Self-control is the ability to live with restraints. Society today
is telling us to let it all hang out, do your own thing, look out for
#1, and to be free of all restraints. If we are to restrain or control

ourselves in the eyes of this world it's only so that we do not abuse someone else. But the Bible goes much further. We are to manifest self-control in order to become like Jesus Christ! It is so that we can experience more and more of His presence and power working in and through our lifestyle. Self-control in reality is a very high form of worship because it is a living out of His commandments — it's a "doing" act of character in order that all of the fruit of the Spirit will be seen in us.

So we have come now to the last of these nine harvests of the Spirit. Taking a line from the "Beatitudes" of Jesus — BLESSED ARE THE SELF-CONTROLLED! Do you find it intriguing that Paul placed this one as last in his listing of the fruit? It's certainly not the least of these. If I were writing these, most likely I would have listed this one as #1 because of its importance and how it relates to the development of the whole gamut of fruit to be harvested. Self-control plays a major role in the maturing of the other fruit in our living. This one provides what is needed to make the other eight operational. Self-control is the glue which holds all of life and all of the harvest of the fruit of the Spirit.

Robert Schuller tells an incredible story of self-discipline in his book, *Move Ahead with Possibility Thinking*. It's about a polio victim who required an iron lung to breathe and learned how to breathe without it, even though every muscle below his Adam's apple is paralyzed. Karl Dewayne Sudekum, through discipline, has learned how to breathe like a frog. Here's the story.

In 1953, while Karl was a lieutenant in the U.S. Navy, he contracted polio. For six years he could breathe only in an iron lung or on a tilt bed. Then he got mad — really angry. He decided he would breathe. He stopped the rocking motion of his bed and remembered how he used to breathe like a frog as a young boy in Nashville, Tennessee. It was a trick almost all kids knew. He would take air with his tongue and force it down his windpipe. When he exhaled, his lungs let out the air like a deflating balloon. He's been breathing this way ever since. "Science doesn't really know how it's done," he said. "It's a two-cycle pumping action that some people can do and some can't. Some people can whistle through their teeth, but I never could. It's like that." He could stay away

self-control is the glue which holds all of life and all of the harvest of the fruit of the Spirit.

from the iron lung as long as he remained awake. With his first real independence, Sudekum decided to become an attorney.

In 1959 he entered the University of San Diego. His wife, Emerald, drove him to school and wheeled him into class. He couldn't take notes and a tape recorder was too awkward. He simply listened and remembered. Then he was told he had diabetes. That under control, the doctors discovered an ulcer. For a year he lived with a mysterious high fever, a reaction to medication. Still, he got his diploma and passed the bar exam.

He is practicing law now and signs documents, K.D. Sudekum. It is too much of a task to write his full name with a pen in his teeth. When he talks too long in court, his face gets very red, but it's nothing to worry about. A cold is something else. It could be fatal. So what does he do? "I don't get colds." If he falls asleep or faints while out on his own, frog breathing, he will die unless someone who knows his condition administers artificial respiration. What does he do about that? "I try to think about it as little as possible."

What a fabulous story of self-control. Now I don't feel so bad about my difficult day. How about you?

Paul the Apostle has written a great passage (1 Cor. 9:24–27) where he likens himself and all of us to athletes who are in vigorous training: "I do not run aimlessly — I beat my body and make it my slave." Pretty strong language in regards to self-control. Nobody said it would be easy. It may be easy to read in concept or principle — but to put it into practice, well that may be something else.

SELF-CONTROL IS . . .

Putting it off doesn't make this any easier. This is one area where we have a desperate personal struggle. Who really is in charge? What life principles will I live by? Who makes the decisions about how life will be lived? These and many more come to mind as we consider our subject at hand. In a major sense, self-control involves the proper use of freedoms. So let's get with it.

Our first study takes us to the writings of Paul as a foundation to all that shall follow this study. Read 1 Corinthians 9:15–27.

What have been your personal motivations for self-control in your past?

_____

_____

_____

_____

What did you grow up with?

_____

_____

_____

_____

What are some of the "rights" Paul is referring to?

_____

_____

_____

_____

What is he referring to when he says, "not make use of my right in preaching"?

_____

_____

_____

_____

How did self-control limit use of rights?

_____

_____

_____

How does self-control limit your use of your rights?

_____

_____

_____

He said, "Though I am free." How does he limit this freedom through self-control so as to further the gospel?

_____

_____

_____

_____

_____

Is there a danger in becoming "all things to all people"? Explain:

_____

_____

_____

_____

How would you go about becoming "all things to all men"?

_____

_____

_____

_____

Why do you think Paul's analogy of being an athlete is good one for the Spirit-filled Christian walk?

_____

_____

_____

_____

How are we to run so as to attain the prize?

_____

_____

_____

_____

What is the "prize" Paul is talking about?

_____

_____

_____

_____

What is the "crown" that will last forever?

_____

_____

_____

_____

Explain what self-control has to do with not "running aimlessly" or "beating the air" wildly:

_____

_____

_____

What does it mean to "beat my body and make it my slave"?

_____

_____

_____

ASSIGNMENT:

• What are the aspects of your own Christian walk which need to be more disciplined?

_____

_____

_____

• What specific steps do you plan to take to insure that they come under more discipline?

_____

_____

_____

_____

CONTROLLING THE TONGUE AND THE BODY

Now we're getting down to the nitty-gritty aspects of where the rubber of self-control really hits the road. We're really getting into meddling in these studies. But how we all need to be reminded of such aspects of the Spirit-filled harvest of character. It's striking the balance of living without restraints in a free society or living as a child of God. It's this very character trait which marks the line of demarcation more sharply than just about anything else between a free-living, undisciplined child of the world and the disciplined lifestyle of a real Christian.

MY KINGDOM

A little kingdom I possess,
Where thoughts and feelings dwell;
And very hard the task I find
Of governing it well.
I do not ask for any crown
But that which all may win;
Nor try to conquer any world
Except the one within.

(Louisa May Alcott)

Please read our passage from James 3:1–12 and 1 Corinthians 6:12–20.

Why is it so difficult to control your tongue?

_____

_____

_____

_____

_____

_____

To whom is James addressing these words?

_____

_____

And — why do you think "teachers" should be held to a higher standard?

_____

_____

_____

_____

How does James say that you may become "a perfect" person?

_____

_____

_____

_____

_____

Why do you think the tongue is considered to be the most uncontrollable part of the human anatomy?

_____

_____

_____

_____

What kind of damage can an uncontrolled tongue cause?

_____

_____

_____

What advice does James give us for controlling the tongue?

_____

_____

_____

_____

Read 1 Corinthians 6:12–20. In your opinion, do you think Christians are more sexually pure than non-Christians are? Why or why not?

_____

_____

_____

_____

What are some of the "permissible" things to which Paul refers?

_____

_____

_____

_____

How is it possible to be "mastered" by these?

_____

_____

_____

What is the underlying principle which Paul lays down when it comes to using the body for any kind of "sexual immortality"?

_____

_____

_____

Why?

_____

_____

_____

_____

When faced with the temptation to commit any kind of sexual immorality, what is the best approach to take?

_____

_____

_____

_____

Why?

_____

_____

_____

_____

If we accept the analogy that the Church is the body of Christ, then if one Christian commits sexual immorality, how does this damage the entire body of Christ?

_____

_____

_____

_____

What life lessons have you gleaned from these two passages?

_____

_____

_____

ASSIGNMENT:

• What aspects of your own personal Christian walk require more self-control and discipline from you?

_____

_____

_____

_____

_____

• What are the steps you plan to take to insure that self-control is applied to each of these areas?

_____

_____

_____

_____

_____

_____

CONTROLLING OUR PASSIONS AND POSSESSIONS

When Demosthenes, the famed Greek orator, spoke the first time in a public setting he was hissed and booed off the platform. His voice was harsh and weak and his appearance was anything but impressive. He determined that his fellow citizens would yet live to appreciate his words, so he practiced day and night.

He shaved half his head so no one would want to invite him to any social events. To overcome a stammer, he spoke with pebbles in his mouth. To build up his voice strength, he went to the seaside and yelled against the rolling thunderous waves of the Aegean Sea.

He stood beneath a sword suspended from the ceiling so as to train him not to slump or favor a shoulder that kept hitching. He practiced his facial expressions in

For the grace of God that brings salvation has appeared to all men. It teaches us to say "No" to ungodliness and worldly passions, and to live self-controlled, upright and godly lives in this present age (Titus 2:11–12).

front of a mirror. It's not surprising that when he next appeared to speak on a public platform, he moved a nation.

He and another orator each were to speak on a particular matter of national concern. When his fellow orator had concluded his speech, the crowd said, "What marvelous oratory." But when Demosthenes finished, they shouted with a single voice: "Let us go and fight Phillip!"

Self-control in action. What about the things in your life — who really is in control or do they control you? This is a most pertinent question to be asking, particularly when it comes to passions and possessions. How are you doing in these areas?

_____

_____

_____

_____

_____

_____

For this next study on self-control, let's begin by reading the biblical passages found in James 4:1–10 and 1 Timothy 6:6–10, 17–19.

What are the things in your life that make you easily angry?

_____

_____

_____

_____

According to the writing of James, what causes people to fight and quarrel with each other?

_____

_____

_____

What are the desires that can cause people to fight and quarrel with each other?

_____

_____

_____

Is it wrong to desire or strive for things that can bring us pleasure?

Explain how friendship with this world can be considered a form of spiritual adultery:

What are the keys that James points out that can help us overcome our passions?

Read 1 Timothy 6:6–10, 17–19. Is it wrong on our part to desire more money and the things that money can buy?

_____

_____

_____

How does the society in which we live help us not to be content only with food and clothing?

_____

_____

_____

_____

Is this a passage that only talks against having more money? Explain:

_____

_____

_____

_____

Is there a difference between having money and the love of money? Explain:

_____

_____

_____

_____

_____

_____

Instead of pursuing money, what does Paul tell us that we should be pursuing?

_____

_____

_____

_____

_____

_____

How can the money or material goods we have be turned into true riches and provide treasure in Heaven?

_____

_____

_____

_____

_____

ASSIGNMENT:

• Are you currently having a struggle with your attitude toward money and what God has to say about money and how to use it? Explain:

_____

_____

_____

_____

_____

What are some specifics you can do to improve any problems you might be having with money and its correct place in your life?

_____

_____

_____

_____

THE MAN WHO LOST SELF-CONTROL AND LOST IT ALL

One of the saddest facts we have to deal with in our day is the frequency with which many "high-profile" Christians have fallen from grace through physical sins. This, however, is not only contemporary to our day. But why? The bottom line is that there is a character flaw, a flaw in the functioning of self-control in a lifestyle. I have a little theory that when the devil is aware of a particularly gifted young person, who is flawed in some aspect of personality, he takes his hands of resistance off and somehow encourages a ministry that becomes popular and high profile. Then at the peak of effectiveness and popularity, the rug is pulled out from under this person and the weakness and sin is exposed for all to see, for all to heap more ridicule upon the Church. We've seen it far too frequently. This is not to say that only high-profile Christians can take a drastic fall — it happens with too much frequency to all.

There are lots of reasons why people fall, why self-control in a particular area is missing. It might be that such people mistake the success they are experiencing with God allowing them some kind of special dispensation in their case. Because God has been blessing, it's also license to indulge self in a secret way. It's a constant vigilance against the world, the flesh, and the devil. Rationalizing is devastating when allowed to happen.

When success of any kind is looked at, you can almost count on it 100 percent that self-control has come into play in some aspect of that person's life. Consider some of these historical figures

Let us be self-controlled, putting on faith and love as a breastplate, and the hope of salvation as a helmet (1 Thess. 5:8).

who, through self-control, have overcome adversity of all kinds: Beethoven, whose best works were composed after he had lost his hearing; Louis Pasteur, whose greatest discoveries were made after he had suffered a life-threatening stroke; John Milton's best poetry came after he was blinded; and William Cowper wrote his greatest hymns following great bouts with deep depression. Self-control is an absolute given if there is to be success of any kind in any person's life — Christian or otherwise.

But what happens when self-control is lost? Our next study takes us to the life of a real he-man with a real she-problem. Read the story in the Old Testament of Samson from the Book of the Judges 16:1–31.

Give some background as to how Samson came to be such a strong man:

Who were judges and how did they function in the life of the nation Israel?

_____

_____

_____

_____

_____

_____

_____

_____

_____

_____

_____

_____

Theological Insight:

The word Nazarite *is from the Hebrew, nazir-elohim, meaning in general one who is separated from certain things and unto others. Specifically it was to be a separation unto Jehovah Eloheim. It could be either male or female and for a lifetime or for a certain specified period of time. The Nazarite was also to be considered the "crowned one." Thus, the uncut hair which was a symbol of vitality and strength. Because this person was to be holy unto the Lord, they wore upon the head the diadem of their consecration in the form of uncut hair.*

What was the meaning and implications to being a "Nazarite"?
(You might want to refer to Judges 13:4–8, 13–14.)

_____

_____

_____

_____

Where and how did the downfall of Samson begin?

_____

_____

_____

Describe the steps of temptation which ultimately caused Samson
to lose his strength?

_____

_____

_____

_____

Why didn't he leave the clutches of Delilah when he surely must have known that she was to be his undoing?

_____

_____

_____

_____

_____

At what point in this whole sad story did Samson actually lose self-control? Why?

_____

_____

_____

_____

_____

_____

Why do you think Samson was so blinded that he allowed himself to be eventually trapped by his sworn enemies?

_____

_____

_____

_____

_____

_____

What do you think was the effect upon his own people, Israel, over whom he was ruler for at least 20 years?

_____

_____

_____

_____

_____

_____

What happens to followers when leaders fail?

_____

_____

_____

_____

What caused the final turnabout in the life of Samson?

_____

_____

_____

What principles of self-control have you discovered in this story
of Samson?

_____

_____

_____

_____

 *ASSIGNMENT:*

• Are there some specific areas in your life where you are most susceptible to the allure of temptation because your self-control is weak?

_____

_____

_____

_____

What steps do you plan to take to shore up these areas of weakness?

_____

_____

_____

_____

_____

_____

THE MAN WHO RULED HIMSELF AND A KINGDOM

In this next study, we'll focus on the positive side of self-control. We'll take another look at a man who controlled himself and eventually also controlled a world kingdom. It's an exciting story!

Joyce Jones is a world-renowned concert organist and organ teacher at Baylor University. Several years ago she was invited to perform the first full concert on the newly installed pipe organ at the Crystal Cathedral in Orange County of Southern California. Let's have a bit of background before we proceed further. At the age of 16 she was a piano major at the University of Texas. But a sprained wrist interrupted her promising career as a pianist. For six weeks she was unable to touch a keyboard. Not wanting to waste any time, she decided to learn to play the organ pedals with her feet, and a new career was born. "God has a way," she relates, "to get your attention and say, 'Hey, I have something better for you to do.'"

Without self-discipline would this have happened? I doubt it. Self-control always has a wonderful payoff. However, at the time of the pain, the payoff may not even be in sight or even thought of. Paul captured some of the pain when he said, "I make my body

The name Daniel *from the Hebrew means: "God is my judge." The Book of Daniel is considered one of the most important prophetical books of the Old Testament. It's an indispensable introduction to New Testament prophecy, which deals with the "times of the Gentiles." This book traces the overview of Gentile world powers down to our present day. And it portrays the ultimate destruction of Gentile world power.*

my slave." Not pleasant, but what a surplus crop to be harvested later.

For our last study on self-control we'll look at a man who lived with self-control and was ready to die if need be to stay with the disciplines of his life. Let's read about this man from his book, Daniel 1:1–21.

How did Daniel come to be in Babylon?

_____

_____

_____

_____

_____

_____

_____

What was his status in Babylon?

_____

_____

_____

_____

_____

Why do you think Daniel "resolved not to defile himself with the royal food and wine"?

_____

_____

_____

_____

_____

_____

What was the food test?

_____

_____

_____

_____

_____

Is this an endorsement for a vegetarian diet? Explain:

_____

_____

_____

_____

_____

_____

Give a description of what kind of a young man Daniel and the other three Hebrews must have been:

_____

_____

_____

_____

_____

_____

Because of their choices, did God bless them?

_____

_____

_____

_____

_____

_____

And how specifically did God bless them?

_____

_____

_____

_____

_____

_____

What are visions and dreams?

_____

_____

_____

_____

_____

_____

What role did self-control and discipline play in these four young men being such outstanding examples of a Christian?

_____

_____

_____

_____

_____

_____

How do we know that self-control was a major part of the lifestyle of Daniel beyond what we have already read in this chapter?

_____

_____

_____

_____

_____

_____

What was the ultimate end of Daniel's ministry?

_____

_____

_____

_____

_____

_____

What lessons on self-control have you learned from the life of Daniel?

_____

_____

_____

_____

_____

_____

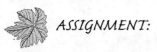 *ASSIGNMENT:*

• Based on our five studies, write your own working definition of
what self-control is and how it functions:

_____

_____

_____

_____

_____

_____

_____

_____

_____

_____

_____

> *I'm a great believer in what I have sometimes called "the daily dogged discipline" of the Christian life. The undisciplined Christian life is a non-productive life. You can't really be a Christian without discipline.*

What in this study of self-control has challenged you the most?

_____

_____

_____

_____

_____

_____

_____

_____

_____

_____

_____

IN SUMMARY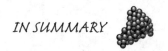

I'm a great believer in what I have sometimes called "the daily dogged discipline" of the Christian life. The undisciplined Christian life is a non-productive life, it's almost an oxymoron. You can't really be a Christian without discipline. If you think it's possible, you must explain it to me. Everywhere I look in the book, I see discipline required as well as the payoff of self-control rewarded. Yes, I know, it's a tough assignment. But without it, how can you ever plan to arrive at the pearly gates of heaven, because on the outside are the undisciplined.

Is it just possible that you have sung these words recently? Even if you have, let's take a disciplined moment to thoughtfully read them:

> TAKE MY LIFE AND LET IT BE
> Take my life, and let it be
> Consecrated Lord to Thee.
> Take my moments and my days,
> Let them flow in ceaseless praise.
> Take my hands, and let them move
> At the impulse of Thy love.

Take my feet and let them be
Swift and beautiful for Thee.

Take my voice, and let me sing
Always, only, for my King.
Take my lips, and let them be
Filled with messages from Thee.
Take my silver and my gold;
Not a mite would I withhold.
Take my intellect, and use
Every power as Thou shalt choose.

Take my will, and make it Thine;
It shall be no longer mine.
Take my heart, it is Thine own;
It shall be Thy royal throne.
Take my love, my Lord, I pour
At thy feet its treasure store.
Take myself, and I will be
Ever, only, all for Thee.
                    (Frances R. Havergal)

Just a cursory moment of reflection causes me to think of how
easy it is to sing a lie and how difficult it might be to be totally

self-controlled in order to bring honor and glory to Him! God help all of us! And He has promised the strength to pull it off. The decision is mine to make, the power to do it comes from Him. Therefore, we all can live a life of self-control, as this fruit of the Spirit is cultivated, then harvested for ourselves as well as for others — and always a tribute for Him.

Our world has been staggered by crime on the rise, the rebelliousness of undisciplined young people, the great disappointments of leadership people, and the moral failures of our society. All can be traced to the root cause of undisciplined lives. Lives that have been committed to doing their own thing or for that matter, not doing anything, period. Why

"Success is not based on where you start, it's where you finish, and I finished! . . . The joy has been the journey!"
(Bob Wieland)

the shattering and breakup of so many "good" homes? Why the violence in home, school, and community? Again, we come to a root-cause breakdown in the disciplines of life. Undisciplined parents give birth to offspring that are even more undisciplined and so the vicious cycle only repeats itself. The tide for self-discipline has risen! There is a crying need for it in all phases of life. Think of what a disciplined people can accomplish. If we are to survive our current age, we must be disciplined by self as well as the Word of God. This final fruit of the Spirit is self-control, self-discipline, temperance, restraint, and directed focus. Isn't it interesting that Paul the Apostle has chosen to conclude his listing with this, the crowning fruit of the Spirit?!!

Bob Wieland finally crossed the finish line on Thursday, November 6, 1986 — the New York City Marathon's 19,413th and final finisher! He was the first ever to run a marathon (26 miles) with his arms instead of his legs.

Wieland, then a 40-year-old Californian whose legs were blown off in a Vietnam battlefield 17 years previously, recorded what race officials said was the slowest time in marathon history: four days, two hours, 48 minutes and 17 seconds!

He was greeted like a champion by race director Fred Lebow, who had written Wieland off as a dropout. When he finished,

Wieland shouted, "We love New York!" and repeatedly pumped his arms into the air. He claimed his finisher's medal and explained why he did it. "For the same reason as 20,000 other people," he said. "It's the greatest marathon in the country."

He then cited three specific reasons: to show his born-again Christian faith, to test his conditioning, and to promote the President's Council on Physical Fitness of which he is a member.

Wieland, whose life is marked by self-discipline, started the race on Sunday at 8:23 a.m., more than two hours before the main body of runners. But moving at an average speed of about one mile an hour, his lead soon vanished. Gianni Poli ran the entire race in the time it took Wieland to cross the Verrazano Bridge. Wieland runs in a sitting position, using his muscular arms like crutches to lift his torso and swing it forward. He sits on a 15-pound saddle and covers his clenched fists with pads he calls "size one running shoes."

Wieland said, "Success is not based on where you start, it's where you finish, and I finished! The first step was the most difficult — after that, we were on our way home. The joy has been the journey!"

There you have it — THE JOY HAS BEEN THE JOURNEY! The payoff in self-control is when you make your way through the gates of Heaven, home. Yes, the journey may be rough, long, and a bit lonely, but with the self-disciplined life, you can be assured that you can finish!

I have fought a good fight, I have finished the race, I have kept the faith. Now there is in store for me the crown of righteousness, which the Lord, the righteous Judge, will award to me on that day — and not only to me, but also to all who have longed for his appearing (2 Tim. 4:7–8).

And the fruit of the spirit is . . . SELF-CONTROL!

Nine Fruits of the Spirit

Study Series includes

Love

Joy

Peace

Patience

Kindness

Goodness

Faithfulness

Gentleness

Self-Control

Robert Strand

Retired from a 40-year ministry career with the Assemblies of God, this "pastor's pastor" is adding to his reputation as a prolific author. The creator of the fabulously successful Moments to Give series (over one million in print), Strand travels extensively, gathering research for his books and mentoring pastors. He and his wife, Donna, live in Springfield, Missouri. They have four children.

Rev. Strand is a graduate of North Central Bible College with a degree in theology.